Over in the Meadow

Adapted by Kate Ruttle and Richard Brown

Illustrated by Rosalind Beardshaw

CAMBRIDGE
UNIVERSITY PRESS

Over in the meadow,
in the sand, in the sun,
lived an old mother turtle
and her little turtle one.

"Dig!" said the mother.
"Let's dig," said the one.
So they dug all day
in the sand, in the sun.

Over in the meadow,
where the stream runs blue,
lived an old mother fish
and her little fishes two.

"Swim!" said the mother.
"Let's swim," said the two.
So they swam all day
where the stream runs blue.

Over in the meadow,
in a big old tree,
lived an old mother squirrel
and her little squirrels three.

"Climb!" said the mother.
"Let's climb," said the three.
So they climbed all day
in the big old tree.

Over in the meadow,
by an old barn door,
lived an old mother mouse
and her little mice four.

"Sleep!" said the mother.
"Let's sleep," said the four.
So they slept all day
by the old barn door.

Over in the meadow,
in an old beehive,
lived an old mother bee
and her little bees five.

"Buzz!" said the mother.
"Let's buzz," said the five.
So they buzzed all day
by the old beehive.

Over in the meadow,
in a nest made of sticks,
lived an old mother blackbird
and her little blackbirds six.

"Sing!" said the mother.
"Let's sing," said the six.
So they sang all day
in the nest made of sticks.

Over in the meadow . . .

can you find everyone?

Over in the meadow,
in the sand, in the sun,
lived an old mother turtle
and her little turtle one.

"Dig!" said the mother.
"Let's dig," said the one.
So they dug all day
in the sand, in the sun.

Over in the meadow,
where the stream runs blue,
lived an old mother fish
and her little fishes two.

"Swim!" said the mother.
"Let's swim," said the two.
So they swam all day
where the stream runs blue.

Over in the meadow,
in a big old tree,
lived an old mother squirrel
and her little squirrels three.

"Climb!" said the mother.
"Let's climb," said the three.
So they climbed all day
in the big old tree.

Over in the meadow,
by an old barn door,
lived an old mother mouse
and her little mice four.

"Sleep!" said the mother.
"Let's sleep," said the four.
So they slept all day
by the old barn door.

Over in the meadow,
in an old beehive,
lived an old mother bee
and her little bees five.

"Buzz!" said the mother.
"Let's buzz," said the five.
So they buzzed all day
by the old beehive.

Over in the meadow,
in a nest made of sticks,
lived an old mother blackbird
and her little blackbirds six.

"Sing!" said the mother.
"Let's sing," said the six.
So they sang all day
in the nest made of sticks.